PLANTS

Forest Plants

Ernestine Giesecke

Heinemann Library
Chicago, Illinois

Designed by Depke Design
Illustrations by Eileen Mueller Neill
Printed in Hong Kong by South China Printing Co. (1988) Ltd.

04 03 02
10 9 8 7 6 5 4 3

Library of Congress Cataloging-in-Publication Data

Giesecke, Ernestine, 1945-
    Forest plants / Ernestine Giesecke.
      p. cm. – (Plants)
    Includes bibliographical references (p.) and index.
    Summary: Describes how various plants adapt to living in a forest,
including the skunk cabbage, maple tree, and dogwood.
    ISBN 1-57572-823-0 (lib. bdg.)   1-4034-0528-X (pbk. bdg.)
    1. Forest plants—Juvenile literature. [1. Forest plants.]
I. Title. II. Series: Plants (Des Plaines, Ill.)
QK938.F6G485 1999
  581.73—dc21
98-45520

                    CIP

AC

Acknowledgments:

The Publisher would like to thank the following for permission to reproduce
photographs:
Cover: Dr. E.R. Degginger
Dr. E.R. Degginger pp. 2, 4-5, 8-11, 13-14, 16, 17, 27; Patti Murray/Earth Scenes
pp. 12, 25; Peter Arnold p. 16; John Lemker/Earth Scenes p. 18; Carson
Baldwing, Jr./Earth Scenes p. 19; Glenn Oliver/Visuals Unlimited p. 20; Michael
Gadomski/Earth Scenes p. 21; Richard Shiell/Earth Scenes pp. 22-23, 26; C.C.
Lockwood/Earth Scenes p. 24; N.M. Stone/Earth Scenes p. 28; Garry D.
McMichael/Photo Researchers p. 29.

Some words are shown in
bold, **like this.** You can find
out what they mean by
looking in the glossary.

CAUTION!
Be sure to take an adult with you when you go exploring
in a forest. Stay away from plants that look like this poison
ivy plant. It can make you feel itchy and uncomfortable.

Contents

The Forest

Some forests have plants that keep their leaves all year. In other forests, called **deciduous** (dee-SIH-joo-us) forests, most of the trees lose their leaves in winter. This type of forest is home to many kinds of tall trees, short plants, flowers, and animals.

The forest plants and animals grow and
thrive in spring and summer. In fall, they
begin to get ready for the long cold
winter. Some plants will die. Some
animals will sleep until spring.

Forest Plants

Oak Tree

Maple Tree

Trout Lily

May Apple

Skunk Cabbage

Fern

In spring, sunlight reaches the forest floor.
Many plants **sprout** and grow in the
spring sun. Soon summer comes and the
trees are full of leaves. The leaves form
a **canopy** that acts like a roof.

Choke Cherry

Chestnut Tree

Virginia Creeper

Dogwood

The canopy stops the sun from reaching the forest floor. Few plants can grow in the shade of the trees. But plants can grow in the sunny places along the edge of the forest.

Skunk Cabbage

Visit a forest in late winter and you will see skunk cabbage. It is one of the first plants to push up through the **soil.**

Skunk cabbage looks a little like the
cabbage you eat. When it is picked,
it smells awful. That's why it is called
skunk cabbage.

9

Fern

Ferns grow well in **damp** forest areas.
In early spring the curly stem of this fern
appears. It looks like the end of a fiddle.
It is called a fiddlehead.

Ferns are plants that do not have flowers.
The brown **spores** on this fern will
someday grow into new ferns.

May Apple

The may apple takes only a few days in spring to push through the forest **soil**. Then it begins to unfold its leaves.

Once its leaves are open the may apple looks a little like an umbrella. You must look under the leaves to see the may apple flower.

Trout Lily

The trout lily and the other forest plants
have to make their flowers, fruits, and
seeds quickly. They need to finish growing
while the warm spring sunshine can still
reach the forest floor.

The trout lily makes extra food in spring. It stores the food underground. This food keeps the plant alive so that it can send new **shoots** up next spring.

Oak Tree

The oak tree is a tall plant with a single woody stem called a trunk. The tree has a **crown** of leafy branches. They form part of the forest **canopy.**

When spring comes, you can see many buds on oak trees. The buds will open and the leaves inside will grow.

Chestnut Tree

This chestnut tree is a large flowering plant. Its flowers, called **catkins**, hang from the branches of the tree.

After the chestnut tree flowers, a tiny seed
is formed. The seed grows throughout the
summer and by fall it is a fully-grown
chestnut—ready to eat or grow into a
new tree.

Maple Tree

The leaves of this maple tree contain green **pigments** called **chlorophyll** (KLOR-uh-fill). Chlorophyll helps trees turn water and sunlight into food for the maple tree.

Maple leaves contain many colors besides
green. In fall, the chlorophyll breaks
down. Then we get to see the other colors
in the leaves.

Chokecherry

By early summer, the forest trees have all their leaves. The forest floor is shaded. Forest plants like this chokecherry need sunshine. They grow at the outer edge of the forest.

These white flowers will make dark red
fruit that birds and other animals eat.
They scatter the chokecherry's seeds in
their droppings. This is one way new
plants can grow in different places.

Virginia Creeper

This Virginia creeper is a **vine.** It has
tendrils along its branches. The tendrils
help the vine cling to trees and bushes
where it can get the light it needs to grow.

The Virginia creeper has blue-black
berries. The berries are related to the
grapes you eat, but do not eat them!

Dogwood

This dogwood is part of a tangle of bushes
and **vines** that live at the edge of a forest.
In fall the leaves of this dogwood turn purple.

Dogwood **shrubs** also grow at the edge of the forest. In summer, the dogwood has small white flowers.

The Forest's Future

For many years, people have cut down forests to make way for roads, towns, and cities. Recently people have begun to replant the trees they cut down.

This may replace some of the lost trees, but it does not replace the forest **habitat**. The smaller plants and the animals that lived in the forest do not always survive even if trees have been replanted.

Glossary

canopy   the highest spreading branchy layer of a forest

catkin   long, slender line of flowers

chlorophyll   thing that makes plant leaves green

crown   leaves and branches at the top of a tree

damp   slightly wet

deciduous   type of tree which loses its leaves in fall and winter

habitat   place where a plant or animal normally lives

pigment   something that makes things have color

shoots   new plants that grow up through the soil

soil   ground that plants grow in

shrub   low plant with several woody stems

spore   part of some plants that can make new plants

sprout   begin to grow

tendril curly part of a plant that helps it cling to things

thrive   to grow strongly

vine   plant with stems that need support

Parts of a Plant

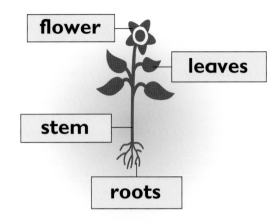

More Books to Read

Fowler, Allan. *Our Living Forests.* Danbury, CT: Children's Press. 1999.

Greene, Carol. *Caring for Our Forests.* Springfield, NJ: Enslow Publishers, Inc. 1991.

Krupinski, Loretta. *Into the Woods: A Woodland Scrapbook.* New York: HarperCollins Children's Books. 1997.

Llamas, Andreu. *Plants of the Forest.* Broomall, PA: Chelsea House Publishers. 1995. An older reader can help you with this book.

Morris, Neil. *Forests.* New York: Crabtree Publishing
Company. 1998.

Stone, Lynn M. *Woodlands.* Vero Beach, FL: Rourke
Corporation. 1996.

Index